REALES ALCAZARES DE SEVILLA (Seville's Royal Palace)

Text, photographs, lay-out and reproduction, entirely designed and created by the Technical Department of EDITORIAL ESCUDO DE ORO, S.A.

2nd Edition, May 1991

I.S.B.N. 84-378-1317-4

Dep. Legal B. 19877-1991

editorial escudo de oro, s.a. Palaudarias, 26 - 08004 Barcelona - Spain

Impreso en España - Printed in Spain
F.I.S.A. Palaudarias, 26 - 08004 Barcelona

Joaquín Romero Murube Street.

SEVILLE

Seville stands on the banks of the river Guadalquivir, called *Betis* by the Romans. The city lies in the midst of a flat area almost devoid of geographical features, under a clear sky of unbroken matchless blue.
Present-day Seville owes its structure to the Middle Ages, built to avoid the summer heat. The result has been a surprising maze of small squares and narrow streets with some striking vistas.
Nestling among them are whitewashed houses decorated with a riot of coloured flowers; their inner courtyards are an Andalusian adaptation of the Roman and Eastern inheritance.
However, if we want to trace the origins of the city back in time we have to hark back further than the Middle Ages. The original name of the city was *Hispalis,* indicative of Iberian or Phoenician roots. It was later totally Romanized, and during the Arab occupation its privileged geographical position, together with its river, the Guadalquivir (from the Arabic, meaning 'large river') navigable up to the district of Triana, made it a city of the greatest importance for the emirs. It reached the high-water mark of its splendour during the latter days of Moslem power, as is shown by the unmistakable outline of the Giralda tower.
In 1249 Seville was conquered by King Ferdinand III, who made the city his court residence, and from that date on it became a favourite place for Christian

The Lion Gate, main entrance to the Reales Alcázares.

The Hunting Courtyard, seen from the Lion Courtyard.

The Plasterwork Courtyard.

monarchs such as Alfonso X, Peter I, the Catholic Monarchs, and the Emperor Charles V. After the discovery of America, Seville was given the task of supervising shipping with the New World and the remains of Christopher Columbus were brought to the cathedral.

Seville has not only been important from the historical point of view. Its contribution to general culture and the arts has been equally impressive. Seville was the birthplace of Antonio Nebrija, the author of the first Spanish grammar. Painters born here were Velázquez, Murillo and Zurburán. Poets such as the Romantic Bécquer, the Machado brothers, Vicente Aleixandre and Luis Cernuda complete the list.

SEVILLE'S REALES ALCAZARES

Seville's Alcázar (citadel or palace/fortress) also goes by the name of Reales (Royal) Alcázares, and is one of the most beautiful buildings in this capital of Andalusia. Its attraction derives both from its great age and the different architectural styles gradually introduced with the passage of time.

The history of its building is intimately linked to and follows the vagaries of the history of the city in which it was built.

The cluster of buildings today known as the Alcázar is basically Arab in design, though later it was to undergo sweeping reforms as well as having independent buildings raised inside.

Coffering in the Hall of Justice.

The origins of the Alcázar are unknown. It is believed to be located on the site of the old Roman citadel which already existed during the times of the caliphate. One thing is certain, however, and that is that building was carried out during the times of the petty kings, who used it as a place of residence, as did the Almohad dynasty, which reached Seville in the 12th century.
The Arab Alcázar survived intact to the times of Ferdinand III, who established himself there, dying in 1252.
Later his son and heir Alfonso X 'the Wise' carried out substantial reforms, which would explain the markedly Gothic character of some of the sections of this original Alcázar, known as the Old Alcázar.
In the 14th century the legendary King Peter I of Castile built the new palace (called 'al-kzar' in Arabic) which bears his name and which has been incorporated into later buildings, thus changing the original design.
King Peter brought in the best architects, artists and craftsmen of his day. Together they created a splendid example of Mudejar architecture in which there is a perfect interplay of Arab and Christian art.
Basic building continued on into the reigns of John II and the Catholic Monarchs, who received Christopher Columbus in this palace when he requested financial help to carry out his mission of finding a new trade route to the Indies.
On the occasion of the betrothal of the Emperor Charles V to Princess Isabella of Portugal, a first floor was added to the Alcázar; general improvement was also carried out, introducing elements of Renaissance in some of the rooms, and building pavilions in the gardens. Of the latter, that known as the Emperor's pavilion still stands.
After this protracted period of practically uninterrupted building until the 16th century, the Alcázar underwent further modifications, on some occasions due to the taste in art matters of the times, and on others because of the need for restoration in certain parts of the buildings. These modifications were not always for the good of those areas occupied by the original Arab buildings.
Since the times of the Emperor to the present day, the Alcázar has continued to be the temporary or summer residence of Spanish monarchs.
In the itinerary suggested on the following pages, a fuller and more detailed description of the buildings and gardens forming the architectural ensemble of the Reales Alcázares of Seville will be provided.
The order proposed does not follow the chronological order of building, but rather a more natural one, passing from salons to buildings to gardens to courtyards, which the visitor is likely to encounter.

PUERTA DEL LEON

The 'Lion Gate', the main access point to the enclosure of the Reales Alcázares, stands in the Plaza del Triunfo.
The name of this gate comes from the magnificent glazed tilework heraldic lion over the lintel. It supports a cross with the legend "ad atrumque" in its right paw.
This tilework lion dates from the 14th century and was restored in the 19th. It symbolises the triumph of the Christians over the Arabs, thus seen in an animal whose traditional virtues are strength and courage.
This gate was once known as the Hunting Gate (Puerta de la Montería), taking its name from the courtyard to which it afforded access.

PATIO DE LA MONTERIA, SALA DE JUSTICIA AND THE PATIO DEL YESO

The 'Hunting Courtyard' gets its name from the fact that it was a meeting place for the nobles and huntsmen who accompanied the various monarchs in the chase.
Next to the Hunting Courtyard stands the 'Hall of Justice', which, according to Torres Balbás, was built in the reign of Alfonso XI.
It is square in shape, with three arches on each side and windows on the upper part. Most of the walls are covered with plasterwork in the shape of coats of arms with castles and lions as well as others of the Order of the Sash, established by Alfonso XI on the occasion of the battle of El Salado (1340).
The ceiling has richly-worked Mudejar coffering. In the centre of the room there is a fountain linked by means of a small channel to the pool of the Patio del Yeso.
The 'Plasterwork Courtyard' just mentioned is rectangular with a post-Moslem 12th-century seven-arch arcade on one of its sides.
The central, and largest, arch rests on pillars while the others are supported on columns with caliphal capitals from the palace of Al-Mansur in Al-Zahira.

PATIO DEL LEON

The 'Lion Courtyard' is reached from the Hunting Courtyard via three broad walled (presumably Roman) arcades belonging to the old fortifications guarding the entrance to the Alcázar.
This large parade ground gets its name from the fact that it was used by the Christian kings to keep the caged lions presented to them by the African kings.
A Playhouse (Corral de Comedias) was built here in the 17th century so that the king could enjoy plays in the comfort of his palace.
Once this playhouse had been dismantled, the courtyard thereafter came to look much as it does today.
The front of the Palace of King Peter I of Castile stands in the Lion Courtyard; it is regarded as being the most refined and lavish example of Mudejar architecture extant.
The main front has a large central section done in ashlar and stuccowork; noteworthy in it are the two doorways with flanking indented Mudejar arches, all dating back to the times of King Peter.
The upper galleries have more delicate work done on them, with patterning and ordering reminiscent of the Granada style. The side galleries were built during the reign of the Catholic Monarchs, at the end of the 15th century.
The upper section of the facade is a filigree of brick, stone and glazed tiles, with a daring polychrome larchwood overhang supported by slender pilasters.
Under the overhang there are twenty small arches, a frieze of escutcheons and twenty corbels.
On the facade there is a cartouche of white and blue

Remains of the Roman wall separating the Lion Courtyard from the Hunting Courtyard.

Entry to the Lion Courtyard and front of King Peter's Palace.

The Lion Courtyard seen from the gallery of the Chamber of Commerce (Casa de Contratación).

Façade of King Peter's Palace.

glazed tilework with the inscription written four times in Arabic letters 'He is not the conqueror, only Allah is'.

Bordering the cartouche the following monkish Gothic script inscription appears: 'The most high and noble and most powerful and most conquering Peter, by the Grace of God King of Castile and Leon, had these alcázares and these Palaces built, which was done in the year one thousand four hundred and two'.

Translating the year of the Arab calendar, to which the inscription refers, into our modern one gives the date of foundation as 1364.

CUARTO DEL ALMIRANTE AND THE CASA DE CONTRATACION DE LAS AMERICAS

The 'Admiral's Room' is reached through the large door decorated with castles and lions, standing on the right of the Lion Courtyard. This room gets its name from the fact that Christopher Columbus, once appointed Great Admiral of the Open Sea, resided in it in 1491 while planning the expedition for the first of his voyages to the Indies. With the help of the Count of Cifuentes, Columbus proceeded to contract the three caravels, the crews and material necessary to implement such a great adventure.

In January 1503 Isabella the Catholic founded a Chamber of Commerce (Casa de Contratación) for the Indies in 1503. The institution was destined to control trade with the New World, as can be seen from the inscription whereby the first Governor appointed was one Don Sancho de Matienzo.
These rooms are steeped in historical memories, since it was here that the most important plans related to the discovery and colonisation of America were hatched. Here sea expeditions were organised, such as that led by Juan de la Cosa, the New World's first map-maker, others led by Enciso and Yáñez Pizón, that of Solís to Mexico and that of Mendoza the provincial governor to what would become Buenos Aires; voyages such as those undertaken by Vasco Nuñez de Balboa in quest of the Southern Sea or that of Alvar 'Cowhead' Nuñez, who travelled across Florida on foot and followed the course of the Mississippi.
The Admiral's Room is decorated with rich 17th- and

Main section of the façade of King Peter's Palace.

Altarpiece of the Virgin of the Seafarers.

18th-century tapestries. Some of them take their subject matter from mythology, others from the Bible.
This room leads to the splendid Audience Chamber and the Navigators' Chapel.
The room itself is rectangular and has a magnificent 16th-century wooden coffered ceiling, reminiscent of the Arabs in its geometrical patterns.
The wall of honour holds the retable of the Virgin of the Seafarers, the protectress of all seamen. The picture is the oldest religious depiction of the discovery of America ever painted in Europe.
It is the work of the Seville master Alejo Fernández, who painted it between 1531 and 1536 for this very room.
The picture shows the Virgin protecting a group of native Americans under her mantle. In the foreground appear the most important personages of the times; to the left of the Virgin stands Columbus, a fair-haired gentleman attired in rich raiment, and the Pinzón brothers, his companions in the adventure, with red capes. To the right of the Virgin stands Emperor Charles V, depicted with a royal cape and an expression of nobleness on his face.
On the lower third of the canvas are depicted different crafts of those times, also sailing under the protection of the Virgin.
Thus the canvas marries artistic merit to historical interest in that it provides information of the design of the ships that took part in such earth-shattering events.
On the frieze of the Chapel hang the coats of arms of the Admirals of Castile, from Bonifaz (13th century) down to Admiral Enríquez.
Opposite the Virgin's canvas hangs the coat of arms of Columbus.

THE ROYAL RESIDENCE OR UPPER STOREY

Back from the Lion Courtyard, in the same gallery of columns there begins the great main staircase leading up to the royal residence or apartments built, like most of the upper storey, during the reign of Emperor Charles V.
The staircase is decorated with Renaissance Seville

The Virgin of the Seafarers, by Alejo Fernández (16th century).

The Levi Loggia.

ceramics, the monarch's motto of 'Plus Ultra' ('Ever further') being repeated; this motto was opposed to that of 'Non Plus Ultra', symbolising the fear of sailing beyond Gibraltar before the discovery of America. There are two canvasses on the walls; one of them is by the hand of the Seville artist Francisco de la Roela and depicts the Virgin appearing to a person in prayer. The other picture shows a episode of the Crusades with Godefroi de Bouillon, the hero of the first expedition and first king of Jerusalem (1099), kneeling before two angels on Mount Sinai. The painting is the work of Federizo Madrazo and was commissioned by Luis Felipe; it won a gold medal in the 1901 Paris Exhibition.

The coffered ceiling is of the first water, as are the staircase banisters, a superb example of Seville wrought iron work.

The Saleta

The 'Saleta' or royal antechamber stands on the right of the upper story and is the first room to be visited. Old Spanish royal protocol stipulated that before reaching the place where the audiences were held, one should pass through this Saleta, then the antechamber proper, and in the third place through the chamber, where the meeting was to take place.

It was built by Charles V in the 16th century, but parts of it are earlier: the ceiling is from the times of the Catholic Monarchs (15th century), though it was transferred to the Saleta in 1529. This is the reason why the wooden decoration on the ceiling boasts the emblem of the Catholic monarchs: the yoke, signifying the union of the kingdoms of Castile and Leon, and the arrows symbolising the strength of Christian arms.

The Saleta is usually lavishly decorated and furnished, although decoration underwent changes according to the occupant. This notwithstanding, some splendid tapestries by Teniers and others by Wouvermans may be regarded as forming part of the permanent fittings. This room also affords once of the best overall views of the Alcázar, since from this height there is a broad prospect of gardens, walls and vicinity.

The Oratory of the Catholic Monarchs

Leaving the Saleta, passing through a small square room with an interesting, possibly 15th-century Mudejar coffered ceiling, one reaches the chapel known as the Oratory of Isabella the Catholic.

This oratory or chapel was built in 1504 by the Catholic Monarchs, just before the death of the queen. Traditionally it has always been the private chapel of all later queens to inhabit the Alcázar.

The altar is regarded as being one of the finest pieces of work in the Alcázar. It is the work of the Italian Niculoso Pisano, and in it the artist breaks with the Andalusian crafts tradition of mosaic work, introducing Renaissance, meaning working the tiles with a great freedom of colour and patterns by means of combinations of differently coloured spaces, since the chemical substances used for the colouring did not run together when fired, according to the explanation given by J. Romero Murube, thus converting it into one of the most perfect ceramic styles in the world.

Courtyard of the Castilian-style Assistants' House (Casa del Asistente).

This chapel's reredos is entirely dedicated to Queen Isabella.

With extraordinary tenderness it depicts the Visitation of the Virgin Mary to Her cousin St. Isabella. By looking closely at the tilework, one may see that it depicts the twelve tribes of Israel as well as other figures alluding to Biblical events. The laterals are

Entrance (16th century) to the Oratory of Isabella the Catholic.

decorated with emblems and topics alluding to the Catholic Monarch , and also bear their initials.
Some say that Charles V got married in this chapel, though it would appear to be more likely that the event took place in the chapel which the Emperor had built.
The two striking features of this chapel are the purity of patterns and more specially the delicateness of the colouring.

The Banqueting Hall

Retracing one's steps towards the Saleta, one comes to the Antechamber or 'Furriela' of the banqueting hall with its magnificent 15th-century Mudejar ceiling. The banqueting hall is in fact a spacious rectangular room with side doors opening onto the servants' quarters.
The hall was built by Charles V for his marriage banquet. Since that date monarchs such as Philip IV, Philip V, Joseph I, Isabella II and Alfonso XII have held innumerable banquets and ceremonies there.
On the walls hang two important and valuable sets of tapestries, both comprising eight cloths, all of them in Pompeian style.
One of the sets dates from the 17th century and has a pattern of pairs of barley-sugar columns and large jars.
The other set has smaller tapestries placed between the doors.
The hall is lit by three splendid chandeliers made in the Royal Factory in La Granja; that placed in the middle is a reproduction of Venetian chandeliers.
Along the outside of this hall and adjoining rooms there run balconies affording a splendid prospect of the Ambassadors' Hall.
Adjoining the Banqueting Hall are the Billiard Room and the Smoking Room; though both were built in the 18th century, they have late 16th-century coffered ceilings.
The Smoking Room has been restored and refurbished so that it doubles as an Assistants' dining room.

Oratory of Isabella the Catholic, by Niculoso Pisano (1504).

The Banqueting Hall.

The Royal Family's Apartments

The Banqueting Hall is the hub of the apartments of all the royal families that have resided in the Alcázar throughout the centuries. All the rooms here (sitting rooms, bedrooms, studies or playrooms, the Infantas' and Infantes' rooms and so on) run along either side of the palace and have balconies looking out onto the gardens.

Some of the rooms seem to have been built by Charles V to accommodate some of the guests for his wedding.

Today, though the distribution of the apartments has not changed, the use to which they are put has, according to the needs and wishes of the royal family in residence. For example, one of the rooms is today used as a family dining room.

The room known as the 'Saleta of the Infantes' apartments' contains a magnificent picture by José María Esquivel, and is regarded as being one of this painter's best; it is a portrait of Queen Isabella II and her sister María Luisa Fernanda.

There is also a portrait of Francisco de Asís wearing the habit of Calatrava; another canvas by Parceriza (one of the few he painted) shows the ruins of the Monastery of the Knights Templar in Ceiño de

The Family dining room.

Campo, a building which has since disappeared. The next room contains another two interesting pictures by Parceriza, with Barcelona as a subject matter. One is entitled 'Interior of Barcelona Cathedral' and the other 'View of the Cathedral from the Swan Pond'. There is also an extraordinary tapestry with mythological motifs, by Jan de Raes the Younger of Brussels, from a larger collection of eight tapestries found elsewhere in the Reales Alcázares.
The Infantas' Chamber (Cámara de Infantas) is decorated with pastel paintings, two of them by Bernardo López Piquer, one a portrait of Alfonso XII and the other of the Infanta Isabella; the third painting here is a retable of a small prince dressed in white with the order of the Golden Fleece. The first two date from 1863 and the third 1866.
Two other canvasses (1868) depicting the Infantas María Pilar, María de la Paz and Eulalia, are by Fernando F. Moratón. There is another portrait of Queen Isabella in a mantilla.
Here one also finds the famous portrait of Queen Mercedes, painted by Manuel Cabral Bejarano in only thirty hours.
The bedroom of King Peter I is the oldest room on this floor and was built towards 1350. Tradition has it that the king had his bedroom built on the upper

King Peter's Bedroom.

Isabella II's music room.

storey so as to get away from the damp and cold of the ground floor.
On his second marriage, to Doña María de Padilla, after having repudiated Doña Blanca de Borbón, he wished to have his room in a more sheltered place since Doña María was affected by the cold.
The bedroom is a fine square room with splendid embellishments on the coffering and Mudejar plasterwork, which even today are splendidly preserved, reminding us of the Morisco taste of the monarch.
The rooms furniture includes a dressing table and a silver table which once belonged to Queen Isabella II; they are important examples of the silver and gold work carried on in the 19th century.
King Peter's room is over the Maids' Courtyard (Patio de las Doncellas), opening onto the upper gallery of the same. Over the door lintel leading to the gallery may be seen painted skulls alluding to the legends surrounding the monarch. According to these stories, one of the most famous sentences given by King Peter stipulated that the heads of five Seville judges were to roll, for having been found guilty of accepting bribes concerning their legal judgements.
King Peter was very keen on meting out exemplary punishment for the benefit of his subjects and members of court.
In the gallery giving onto the Maids' Courtyard, there is a portrait by Gonzalo Bilbao of the queen mother María Cristina with her son Alfonso XIII as a boy. There is also a small silver statue of Queen Isabella

Portrait of the Infanta María Luisa Fernanda, by Vicente López.

Isabella II's bedroom.

Isabella II's bedroom, today the office of King Juan Carlos.

II with King Francisco de Asís, their son Alfonso XII and the Infantas Isabella, Paz and Eulalia.
Over the sculpture there is a picture by Genaro Pérez Villaamil, dated 1849, entitled 'Ceremony inside an Arab palace' where the artist gives full rein to his extraordinary imagination.

The Music Room

Going through the gallery and then a service corridor leading to the Royal apartments, crossing the Assistants' Room (some fine large mahogany chests from the times of Ferdinand VII here), one reaches the Music Room ('Sala de Música') alternatively called 'Isabella II's Music Room', since it was built entirely during her reign, having been begun under her father Ferdinand VII.
On the walls there are portraits of Isabella and her family, painted in 1842 by Vicente López, a pupil of Goya's.
One of the portraits shows the queen with a map; another the Duchess of Montpensier, the Infanta María Luisa Fernanda studying solfa. Both were commissioned from Vicente López by Don José Quintana when the latter was tutor to the Infantas.
There are also portraits (second half of the 18th century) of Charles III and his wife Doña Amalia. Also 18th-century is another depicting a lady leaning on a marble column, as is another of a girl dressed in blue with red sash and the Golden Fleece.
The room also has two small trunks bearing the

King Juan Carlos' office seen from the intercolumnation.

signature R.G. Hispaleto. In one of the corners stands a Romantic piano, built by the prestigious Paris firm of Erhard, mid-way through the 19th century.

Isabella II's Bedroom

Isabella II's bedroom stands to one side of the previous room.
Currently it is used as an office by His Majesty King Juan Carlos.
Noteworthy fittings are the bed (taking up a good part of the room), the chandelier and the decoration round the fireplace, which bears the initials of the queen.
Separated by an intercolumnation stands the cabinet or dressing room containing extremely delicately-worked oval portraits in pastel colours depicting Queen Isabella, Alfonso VII, the Infanta Isabella and the Marchioness of Novaliches. There are also numerous enamels, decorative objects and two very interesting pieces of furniture: a dressing table and a mahogany prie-dieu with bronze fittings.
The prie-dieu reproduces a copy of the 'Betrothal of St. Catherine' by Correggio, and the Twelve Apostles, all done in brightly-coloured porcelain and made in the Vatican porcelain factory.

The Audience Chamber

The adjoining room is the Audience Chamber

('Cámara de Audiencias). When describing the Saleta, mention was made of royal protocol and the need to pass through three different rooms before being granted audience. We shall go through those same rooms in the reverse order followed by official visits; firstly we shall visit the Chamber and then the Antechamber.
The Chamber belongs to the reign of King Peter; its Morisco decoration is the richest of all the rooms of the upper storey.
It has walls with Mudejar plasterwork, fantastic glazed tilework and stilted half-point arches resting on rose marble columns.
The Antechamber is generally known as a waiting room for royal audiences. This room was also built in Mudejar style.
Once again in the Saleta, our visit to the upper storey comes to an end. We now go down via the main staircase to proceed to the most legendary part of the Alcázar, King Peter's Palace, whose facade we have already looked at in detail.

KING PETER'S PALACE

King Peter I of Castile is one of the most hotly debated monarchs of Spanish medieval history. Known as 'the Cruel' by some and 'the Justice-giver' by others, he had a special liking for Seville, a city he chose to be his capital and well as the city of his love affairs.
The chronicles record that his was tall and fair, courageous on the battlefield and of unmitigated severity in the meting out of justice. He took a strong stand both against his nobles by drafting the 'Craftsmen's Ordinances' (which protected artisans and workers from the whims of the nobles) and the church (by curtailing the privileges of the high clergy). He was responsible for the death of Don Fadrique, his illegitimate brother, for having committed adultery with his queen Doña Blanca; previously he had heaped honours on him and had granted him the high military rank of Master of the Order of St. James. The king himself was assassinated by conspirators after various years of war against a band headed by his other illegitimate brother Henry of Trastamara, who was to succeed him to the throne.
King Peter wanted to build his own place of residence within the enclosure of Seville's Alcázar; for this purpose he raised a great palace influenced by Moslem architecture, which is now a jewel of Mudejar art. 'Mudejarism' is the name originally applied to those artistic expressions executed by Moslems (Mudejars, hence the name) who lived in the territory reconquered by the Christians, and who submitted to the new government; by extension it also includes work created by Spanish Christians under the influence of Islamic art.
King Peter's palace was built by Toledo craftsmen and master builders from Seville and Granada, the latter being sent by Mohammed V, whom the Castilian king had helped to reclaim his throne in Granada.

The Palace Vestibule

The simplicity and relatively small size of the Vestibule, the first room we find on our visit around this palace, contrasts with the magnificence of the front and gives no idea of the wealth to be found inside the palace proper.
The aim of the Vestibule is to give the visitor a feeling of peace and quiet, similar to what is felt in Arab temples; hence it is devoid of decoration, except for the four columns topped by Classic capitals coming from older buildings, according to Romero Murube. Here there are no fittings whatsoever, although previously there must have been coat-hooks where visitors to the King could relieve themselves of their

King Juan Carlos' office, seen from the Audience Chamber.

The Audience Chamber.

Coffering on the Audience Chamber. ▷

mantles and overcoats before being received by him. A narrow dimly-lit corridor runs from the Vestibule to the bright light and harmony of the palace's great courtyard.

The Maidens' Courtyard

The main courtyard of King Peter's Palace is popularly known as the 'Maidens' Courtyard' ('Patio de las Doncellas'), since tradition has it that the young girls of the royal family and those of the servants together spied through the lattice-work windows on the high dignitaries passing through it to get to the main apartments and the Ambassadors' Hall, where they were received by the king.

The courtyard was built on the orders of King Peter of Castile, and is the most splendid example of a Mudejar courtyard to be found in Spanish architecture.

It is square in shape, and framed by lobed-arch galleries on twin columns, later replaced in the 16th century by others of Italian marble.

From the lobed arches (to be found all over the Alcázar) there begin delicately worked geometric patterns in plaster.

The walls boast a valuable collection of original tilework dating from the 14th century.

The courtyard was later modified by a high, glassed-in gallery during the reign of the Emperor Charles V, which makes it difficult to imagine exactly how the original fortified mansion must have been.

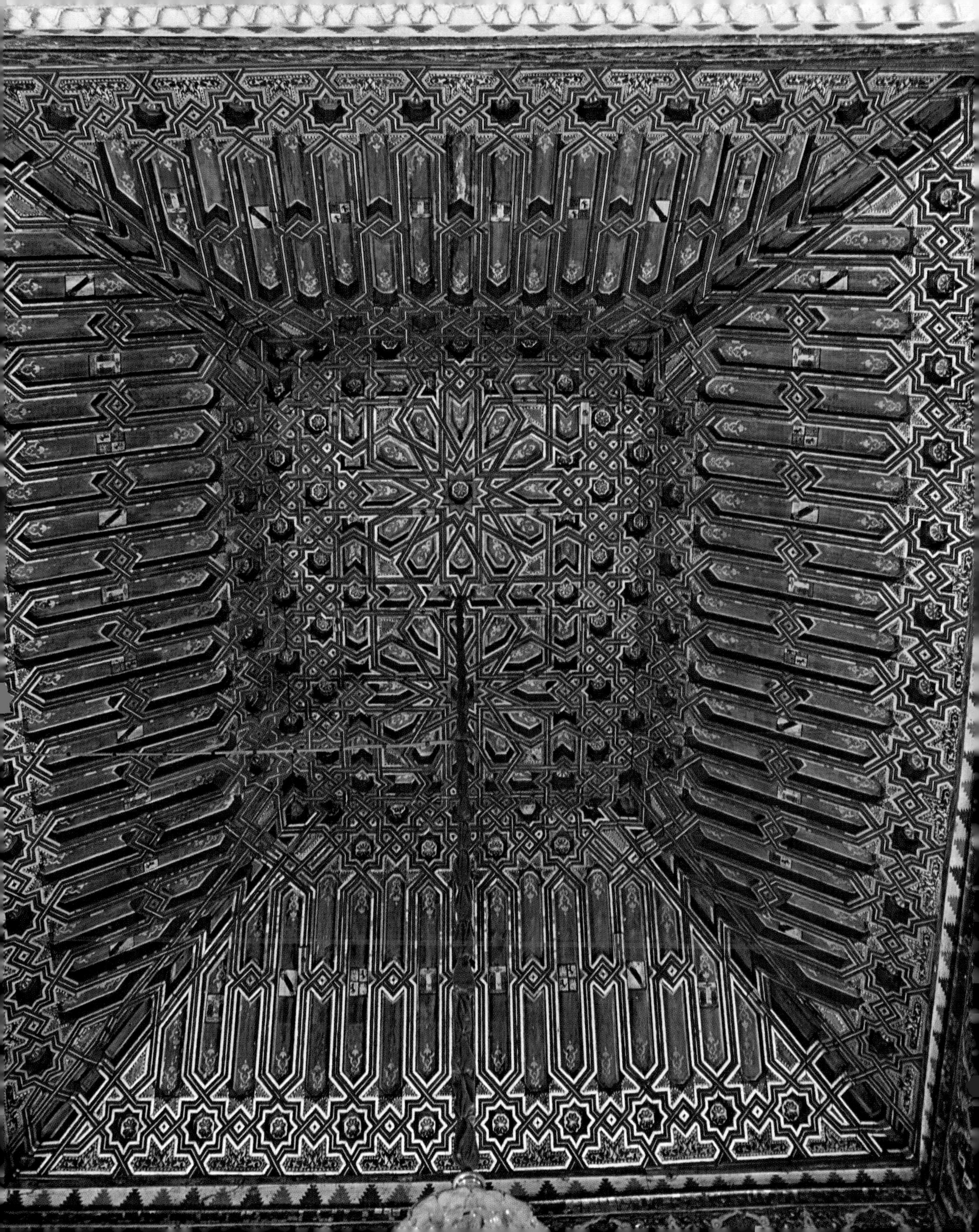

The Antechamber or Waiting Room.

Charles V's Ceiling Room

There are two large salons opening onto the Maidens' Courtyard; one is the Emperor Charles Room, which is located on the main wall side next to the entrance corridor.

This Room is the first of a series of rooms and studies. It gets its name from the splendid Classic coffered cedarwood ceiling which replaced the original Mudejar ceiling during the Emperor's reign. Some of the central coffers display portraits, one of them being presumably Charles V himself and his wife Doña Isabella of Portugal.

In another of the rooms of this part of the palace, a stone indicates the birthplace of the Infanta María Isabella of Orleans and Bourbon, daughter of Isabella II (b. 21st. September 1848).

Then comes a long room running the length of the Ambassadors' Hall; it has a fine wooden ceiling created by Juan of Simancas during the reign of Philip I (15th century).

The rooms ends in a façade of columns with three arches, called the Peacock Arch.

It is decorated with plasterwork and Mudejar patterning with Eastern, possibly Persian, influences. This would account for the peacocks in the corners (from

Vestibule of King Peter's Palace.

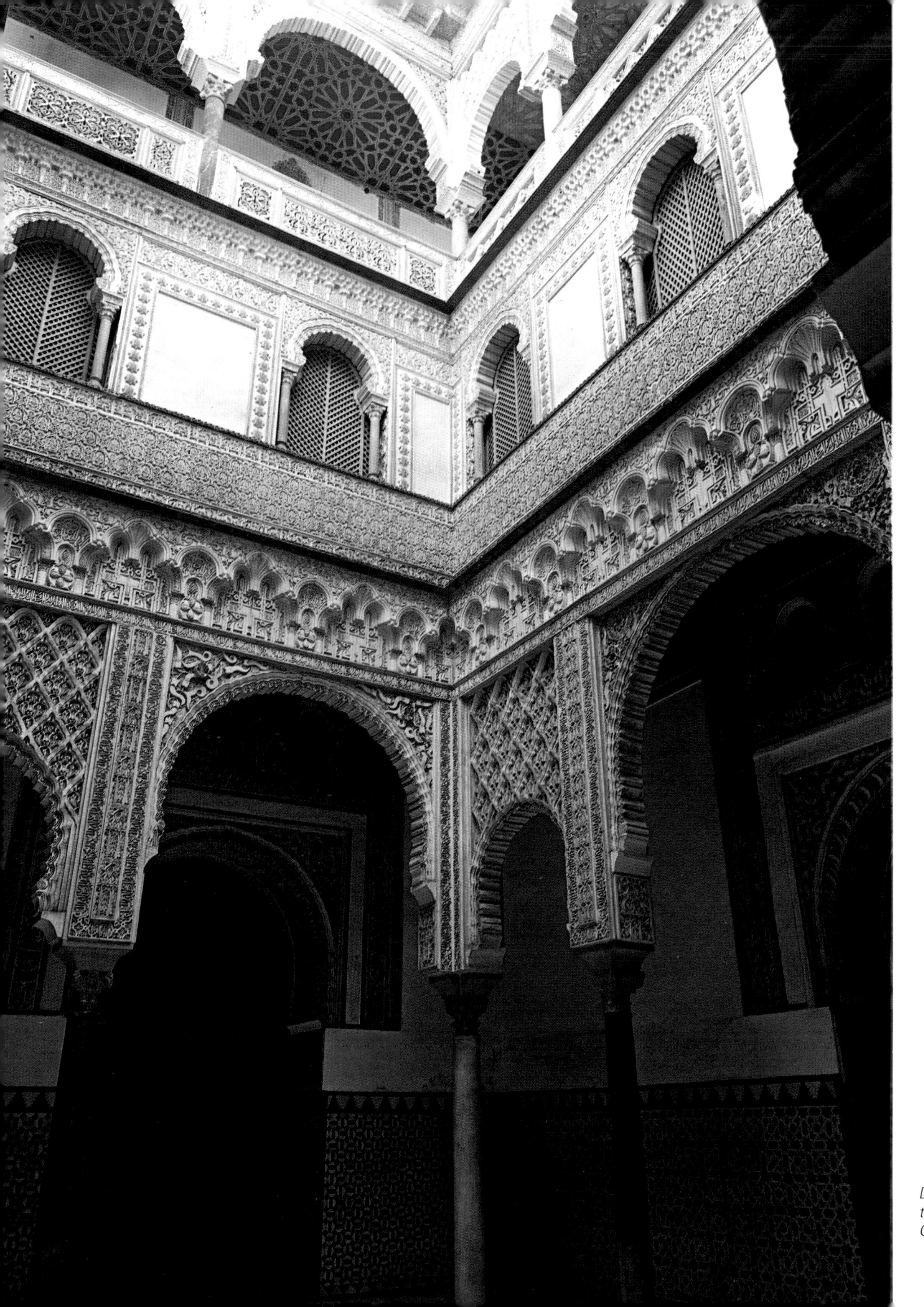

Detail of the Dolls' Courtyard.

The Dolls' Courtyard.

Detail of the coffering in the Prince's Room.

The Peacock Arch, between the Philip II Ceiling Room and the Ambassadors' Hall.

The Ambassadors' Hall.

which the arch takes its name), since Moslem art did not permit flora or fauna motifs, in accordance with the Islamic religion, which prohibits the representation of animals and plants.

The Ambassadors' Hall

This room takes its name ('Salón de Embajadores') from the Arabic inscriptions on the great door affording access to it from the Maidens' Courtyard; they allude to the political use made of the hall, i.e. a reception room for ambassadors and other dignitaries.

It had previously been known as the 'Dome hall' after the splendid semi-circular roof covering it, the interlaced design being the work of the master Diego Ruiz, who finished it round about 1427.

The Ambassadors' Hall is of the jewels in the crown of King Peter's palace, in view of its balanced proportions and the lavish decoration. It is square, has a magnificent Seville glazed tile dado, the walls are covered in strikingly perfect mosaics and plasterwork. On the side walls there are intercolumnations with rich pink marble columns topped by highly worked capitals.

The dome rests on a broad frieze decorated with castles and lions; the supporting squinches still show

The Ambassadors' Hall.

here and there the shine of the gold leaf with which it was once covered. The frieze is followed by a series of arches with portraits of the kings of Spain, from Recaredo to Philip II.
The excellently worked wrought iron balconies on the upper body are from the reign of the Emperor Charles.

The Dolls' Courtyard

From the Ambassadors' Hall one proceeds to the so-called 'Dolls' Courtyard' ('Patio de las Muñecas'). It takes its name from the small female heads appearing on the decoration of some of the arches.
Tradition has it that King Peter had this courtyard built as a playground for his daughters, the adjoining rooms being used as bedrooms and games rooms for them and their servants.
The courtyard is a small, intimate one and of exquisite ornamental delicacy. However, only the ground floor is original since the upper storey was restored last century.
The arch columns are decorated with capitals in different styles and from different times; some of them bear Moslem inscriptions, indicating they are from the times of the Cordoba caliphate.
With the Dolls' Courtyard begins that part of the

The Ambassadors' Hall. Iconographic gallery in the form of a frieze, depicting the Spanish kings from Recaredo to Philip II.

palace intended as private apartments for the royal family; the Maids' Courtyard marked the beginning of the official part of the palace.

The Prince's Room

It is thought that this room was reserved for Don Juan, son of the Catholic Monarchs.
The ceilings of the three sections into which the room is divided are magnificent, as is that of the small bedroom called Isabella the Catholic's Ceiling Room ('Sala del Techo de Isabel la Católica'), which also communicates with the Dolls' Courtyard.

The Bedroom of the Moorish Kings

From the Dolls' Courtyard one reaches another large room popularly known as the Bedroom of the Moorish Kings ('Dormitorio de los Reyes Moros'), though certain scholars believe that 'Moorish' should be left out, since the only kings to use it were Castilian, the adjective being added later in the mistaken belief that the Alcázar was Arab in origin.

THE EMPEROR'S PALACE

Again in the Lion Courtyard, after visiting the María

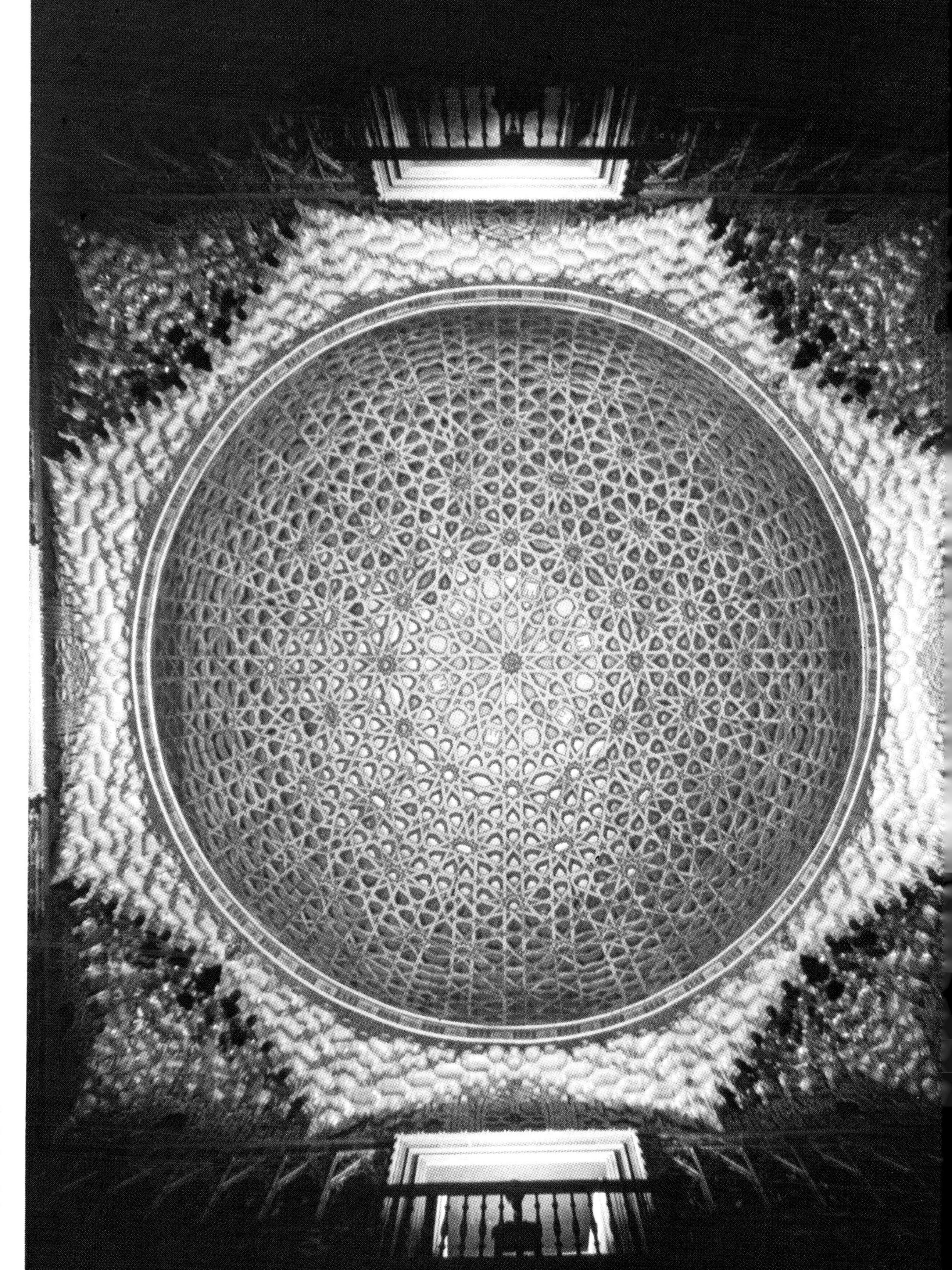

Dome of the Ambassadors' Hall, by Diego Ruiz (1427).

Detail of the Maidens' Courtyard.

Part of the Maidens' Courtyard.

Gothic palace. Chapel known as the ''Emperor's Room''.

de Padilla courtyard (near where tradition places the private rooms of the queen) we proceed to that part of the Alcázar known as the Palace of Charles V ('Palacio de Carlos V') It stands on the site of an older Gothic palace probably raised in the reign of Alfonso X; it is therefore older than King Peter's Mudejar Palace. The building must have originally been a military one, and the layout of some of its sections recalls the style of the Almoravid and Almohad dynasties, though that part now visible is fully Gothic.

Some of the rooms, such as the so-called Baths of Doña María de Padilla, are to be found underground. In fact they are not baths at all but water storage areas or tanks, which popular imagination transformed into the private ablution quarters of the queen. The only Gothic parts which may be visited are the two spacious salons and two side chapels.

The first room's architecture was modified during the 18th century. The room still contains one of the richest Spanish collections of tapestries in existence, that known as the 'Conquest of Tunis by the Emperor Charles V'.

The military expedition to Tunis, undertaken in 1535, was headed by Charles V. Confident in the success of his venture, the emperor took Jan Vermey or Vermayen, his favourite painter, with him to have a record of the most memorable episodes of the struggle.

The painter himself, alternatively known as

Longbeard because of his abundant facial hair, or Jan the Handsome because of his good looks, appears in some of the tapestries, either with the royal entourage or else sketching.

Once the campaign was over, Charles V and his sister Doña María of Hungary, agreed that Vermay should paint the cartoons for the most famous tapestry-maker of the day, Pannemaker, to weave the twelve tapestries with silk, gold thread and wool. The contract stipulated that Charles V would provide the material, so the Emperor had silk brought from Granada, wool from Burgos and the gold from Milan. The work was completed in 1554, and the collection was put on display in the English court on the occasion of the engagement of King Philip to Mary Tudor. Back in Spain, the tapestries provided decoration for the palace ceremonies and solemn occasions. To prevent the originals from damage, in 1740 Philip V ordered the Royal Tapestry Factory in Madrid to make an exact copy of them. This was duly executed in wool and silk, and thanks to this king's foresight we have an idea of what the originals were like, since

Detail of the tilework, by Cristóbal de Augusta (1578).

The Emperor's Palace. The Tapestry Room.

they mysteriously disappeared shortly after being finished, and no one has been able to provide any sort of explanation.
On the upper part of each tapestry in the collection a cartouche in Spanish describes the most important events of the episode depicted; at the foot of each is another text in Latin.

Tapestry 1

This tapestry shows the point of departure (Mediterranean coastline) and arrival (African coastline) of the troops of the Emperor. Curiously enough the map is upside down, with the Iberian peninsula at the bottom and North Africa at the top.
On a cartouche resting on two Corinthian columns the beginning of the campaign is narrated. The figure leaning on the right-hand column is Vermay himself, and the cartouche he holds explains why he has drawn the map this way: "...the painter has observed his duty to his art, bearing in mind the observer (of the map) who sees it from Barcelona, whence sail was set for Tunis. This city stands to the south-east, leaving the north behind over the left shoulder. Based then on this truth, one may better understand the particular details of each of the following tapestries..."

Scene from "The Conquest of Tunis by the Emperor Charles V".

Tapestry 2

This tapestry narrates the arrival of the Emperor and his fleet in Barcelona; it describes the brilliance of the entourage comprising the knights of the Royal House and Court, the departure from the port in the company of the Infante Don Luis and other Portuguese knights who also participated in the expedition.

Tapestry 3

Here we see the disembarkment at the port of Tunis, La Goleta, on 16th June 1535. The Emperor lands in the company of his court and twelve thousand infantry; he storms the three towns in the vicinity, as well as capturing the towers known as the Salt Tower and the Water Tower.
The Emperor sets up camp next to the ruins of ancient Carthage, as described by the Latin inscription on the cartouche at the bottom of the tapestry.

Tapestry 4

A skirmish near La Goleta. The Emperor orders his forces down to the plain to invest the fortress, but the Turks turn the wind (which is raising clouds of

Scene from the series of tapestries "The Conquest of Tunis".

dust) to their favour by throwing sand up in the air with stakes and other instruments to blind their enemies.

The storm dies down unexpectedly and the Spanish arquebusiers corner the Turks, who have no alternative but to take refuge in La Goleta.

Tapestry 5

Here we see the Turks sally forth from La Goleta, killing some Italian soldiers and the Count of Sarno, and later the Italian colonel, the Marquis of Final. The Spanish counterattack draws forth a response of four hundred horsemen of the Turkish army under the command of the King of Tunis himself, Mulay Hassan.

The lance-wound received by the Marquis of Mondéjar has the Emperor himself come with reinforcements, forcing the Turks to take refuge in La Goleta, abandoning part of their artillery in the flight. The bottom cartouche says: "The Turks find a way out, throwing back the Italian advances, and taking prisoner first of all their commander, they take the trenches. But they are repulsed by the Spanish, and retreat. Later, trusting in the cover of darkness, they return to the assault on the Spanish, forcing them to abandon the trenches. The latter counterattack, and the former in turn are forced to retreat. King Hassan comes on the scene with a small entourage.

Wounded, Marquis Luis leaves the combat. Charles comes to his succour, when his forces were sore pressed, and repels the enemy, capturing his guns.''

Tapestry 6

This tapestry described one of the most violent encounters of the campaign. The Marquis of Alarcón is attacked by the Turkish army while fetching fodder for his horses and is quickly surrounded. In view of the Marquis' plight, the Duke of Alba goes in to help. The fighting was so ferocious that the Spanish army suffered a great many casualties.

The translation of the Latin text says: ''Then, on the orders of the Duke of Alba, they sally forth in much greater strength to fetch the victuals, which they had sought before in such great danger and such small numbers. They approach the trenches of the fort. The enemy, sallying forth, once more lets fly his arrows against the Spanish. The latter, in a flood of fury that inflames their onslaught, leave the work they have begun and launch themselves headlong against the enemy and pursue them. In their wrath they fight under the very fortifications of La Goleta. When they retreat from the fortress, they suffer many casualties''. The cartouche reads as follows: ''It must be borne in mind that this sixth tapestry must be imagined as looking from the aqueducts going to the cape of Carthage. Of the places in it, Tunis stands on the right hand and the north to the left, looking at La Goleta from the right''.

''The taking of La Goleta'', from the series ''The conquest of Tunis''.

''The conquest of Tunis''. Tapestry.

''The conquest of Tunis''. Tapestry. ▷

Tapestry 7

Here we are told of the taking of La Goleta.
The Spanish army launches an attack by land with eleven cannon while the nine galleons under the command of the Admiral Prince Doria fire salvoes from the sea. La Goleta is defended by six thousand Turks, two thousand Moors and four hundred artillery pieces. The city finally falls, since a corps of four thousand seasoned soldiers from the Spanish Old Infantry Regiment, another four thousand Italian troops, plus two thousand Germans, all join the fray.
The Latin text reads as follows: ''The garrison guarding the watchtower is engaged in an attack launched against it by the Africans. The Caesar comes with help and repels the attackers. La Goleta is harried by land and by sea. But the enemy also fights doggedly with his missiles. A part of the wall crumbles, exactly that part where the fighting is thickest. The Spanish forces are the first into the breach. Having taken it they kill or frighten off the defenders, while Charles is engaged with the remainder of the enemy''.
The cartouche reads: ''It must be supposed that this seventh scene is viewed from the tin mine, with Tunis on the right, and the cape of Carthage on the left. North is behind to the right''.

Tapestry 8

The translation of the Latin reads thus: ''Charles, fill-

Naval battle at La Goleta (''The conquest of Tunis''). ▷

VRBE IVBET CAESAR DECEDI AC MOENIA LINQVI
AGMINE DEDVCTO RADAM CONTENDIT IBIQVE
CASTRA LOCAT. SEQVITVR MOX PRAEDA MILES ONVSTVS.
DAT VENIAM POENO CVNCTIS IN CASTRA VENIRE
VT LICEAT PROPERAT RAMIS INSIGNIS OLIVA
TVRBA CAPVT, QVERITQVE SVOS MINIMOQ. RED
VENDICAT AST ALII QVOS LVCRI CERTA CVPID
TRAXIT PARVO EMPTAS MERCES VESTEMQVE
ORTAT

"The conquest of Tunis". Tapestry.

ed with rage, leads his banners against Tunis. While he takes a suburb, captives make signs from the citadel: by tunneling through the walls and bursting open the gates, they had, with the help of Christ, managed to escape. They had put the garrison to flight and taken the citadel, and are beseeching the avenging Charles to come to their aid. Heraldin flees. The Caesar breaks through the gates, enters the city and claims it as his".

Tapestry 9

Here we see the sacking of Tunis. When done the Emperor returns the King of Tunis to power, making him a tributary king, and protecting him from the tyranny of the Turks.

Tapestry 10

The lower cartouche reads: "When the Caesar returned to La Goleta and his main camp, he ordered the port's fortifications to be rebuilt and entrusted it to a Spanish garrison.
He strikes an alliance with the African, taking him into his friendship and establishing an annual tribute to be paid by himself and his successors. After demobilising the main part of his forces, who then left with the fleet bound for home, he returns to Trapani with his veterans".

Tapestry 11

The Emperor decides that the Tunisians should have their belongings returned to them which had been taken by the Spanish soldiers, in return for being paid a fair price.
The cartouche relates: ''The return of the army to Rada, after the occupation of Tunis, which lasted for eight days. The Emperor disposes that the Moors should go and rescue their wives and children and buy the clothes back from the Spanish soldiers who had taken them during the sacking of the city; in order to be recognised, they are to place olive twigs on their heads.
Finally, the Christians saved from captivity should be provided with ships in order to return to their respective countries according to their nationalities''.

Tapestry 12

With the disappearance of the original tapestry number 8, the subject matter was repeated, and this tapestry is the result. It should therefore be placed

''The conquest of Tunis''. Tapestry.

Pond with a Mercury by Diego Pesquera (1576) and the Grotesque Gallery.

between the current tapestries 7 and 8. It would appear that the original eighth tapestry of the series disappeared when King Philip V ordered the whole collection to be transferred to Madrid for reproduction.
The current number 12 was woven in the Royal Tapestry Factory between 1730 and 1740, and depicts the battle won by the Spanish forces against the Turkish general Redbeard near the wells of Tunis. An extract from the main cartouche reads: "The Emperor marches on Tunis with his army. The order for battle is given and his troops obey. A victory achieved against Redbeard at the Wells, six hundred of the enemy being killed".
After leaving the Tapestry Room, we cross the Emperor's Room with its glazed Triana tilework, the work of the master Cristóbal de Augusta in the 16th century.

THE ALCAZAR'S GARDENS

The different gardens in the Reales Alcázares are renowned for their beauty.
The Moslem gardens lead to Renaissance gardens, which in turn lead to more modern ones.
From the strictly archaeological point of view these gardens have not preserved their original design, but have certainly not lost one whit of their original charm all down the centuries.
Passing through the entrance gate, the first of the gardens one finds is a magnificent Renaissance

The Mercury Pond and the Grotesque Gallery.

garden, which is almost all taken up by a large pool, going by the name of 'Mercury's Pool' ('El Estanque de Mercurio'), since a bronze statue of that god stands in the centre on a splendid bowl decorated with cherubs and figureheads; the statue was apparently cast in 1576 by Bartolomé Morel after a design by Diego Pesquera.

To one side of the pool, on one side of the old wall, is the Grotesque Gallery ('Galería del Grutesco'), decorated in the 17th and 18th century with rough stonework in the shape of grotesques and arcades on the upper part. The ensemble is reminiscent of Italianate which stands in surprising contrast with the wall.

The Grotesque wall acts as a dividing wall between the old gardens on the right and the modern ones. A two-flight eighteenth-century staircase leads down to the Dance Garden ('Jardín de la Danza'), so-called because of the two lead statues of a nymph and satyr, both atop tall columns and ready to take the first steps of their dance.

To the right lie the 12th-century ill-named Baths of Doña María de Padilla, which were in fact an underground water cistern for the Intersection Gardens ('Jardines del Crucero'). These "baths" have ribbed vaults.

The Intersection Gardens lie for the most part over underground galleries, and correspond to the oldest part of the palace premises of the Alcázar which dates from the 9th century.

During the 12th-century Almohad domination, they underwent substantial reform. Today large-scale

Garden in the Huerta del Retiro or the Poets' Garden.

The Fountain Garden.

restoration is under way to restore them to their former shape.

The Prince's Garden

In chapter 23 of the 'History of the Catholic Monarchs Fernando and Isabella' by the chronicler Don Andrés Bernaldez, we read the following: ''On the thirtieth day of the month of June in the year one thousand four hundred and seventy eight, between the tenth and eleventh hours of the day, did the Queen Isabella bear a son, a prince and heir, within the Alcázar at Seville''.
This garden was created for the entertainment and recreation of that Prince.

The Maze

This maze ('Laberinto') dates back to the times of Charles V and only parts of a much larger construction have survived.
Nonetheless, the pool, the fountain and the actual layout of the maze, via which it is possible to trace one's way in and out, can still be appreciated.
Terracotta monsters' heads and gracefully fanciful water leaps appear from time to time in the greenery.

The Ladies' Garden

The Ladies' Garden ('Jardín de las Damas') is also known as the Orange-grove Garden ('Jardín del

The Ladies' Garden.

Overall view of the Charles V pavilion and a detail of the same.

Gardens of the Maze.

Garden in the Huerta del Retiro or the Poets' Garden.

The Marchena Gate, from the family seat of the Dukes of Arcos and Osuna.

The Marchena Gate, at the entry to the gardens of the Reales Alcázares.

Naranjal'), where the orange-trees are said to be the original ones planted during the reign of King Peter. The garden was re-planned by Charles V on the occasion of his marriage to Isabella of Portugal.
Admired by all who visit it, the Italian Andrea Navaggiero said of it on his return to Venice: "There is no more delightful place in the whole world than the gardens of the Alcázar in Seville, for ever covered in orange blossom".
Here stands the Lion Fountain ('Fuente del León') with the Charles V Pavilion behind, built on the occasion of his marriage. The latter is square with a coffered ceiling, a frieze and plasterwork, together with a 16th-century Seville glazed tile dado. The flooring is original, and on it can be read the name of the architect Juan Hernández, who built it in 1543. Beside one of the windows the plan of the original Maze is preserved, thus making reconstruction possible.
On the outside of the Pavilion there is a porticoed porch with half-point arches resting on columns. A whole range of traditional Spanish architectural features were used in the building, mainly in the tilework, which combines heraldic motifs, centaurs, fauns, unicorns and so on.

OTHER SPOTS

That part of land originally taken up by the gardens of the Alcoba and the Alcobilla is now a modern

Patio de Banderas.

English-style garden with a lawn and a park. Behind the Grotesque Gallery there is another stretch of new gardens. The Marchena Gate, taken from the palace of the Duke of Arcos in Marchena, affords access to the gardens known as the Garden of Retreat ('Huerta del Retiro').

On the instructions of Alfonso XIII, this gate was transferred to its present site in 1913. It is a splendid example of late Gothic.

Next to the easternmost wall of the medieval enclosure stands the China Pavilion ('Pabellón de la China'). It is a relatively modern building, the exact date of construction not being known, but the style is that of the early 18th century. It has iron gates and railings dating back to the times of Philip V, whose coat of arms can be seen on the front. Its name comes from the fact that in it were kept the chinaware services for banquets and parties held in the Reales Alcázares, up until the beginning of this century.

Coming to the end of our visit of the Alcázar, we pass through a vast corridor called the Halt ('Apeadero') where the luxurious carriages would stop when Philip V set up his Court in Seville for a period of time. From here we reach the ancient Parade Ground ('Patio de Banderas'), where the troops would parade before going off to war. Just to the right of the exit gate may be seen a small chapel in the wall, before which Columbus prostrated himself before sailing off on his quest to the Indies.

Contents

Collection ALL EUROPE

		Spanish	French	English	German	Italian	Catalan	Dutch	Swedish	Portuguese	Japanese	Finnish
1	ANDORRA	•	•	•	•	•	•					
2	LISBON	•	•	•	•	•				•		
3	LONDON	•	•	•	•	•					•	
4	BRUGES	•	•	•	•	•		•				
5	PARIS	•	•	•	•	•					•	
6	MONACO	•	•	•	•	•						
7	VIENNA	•	•	•	•	•						
8	NICE	•	•	•	•	•						
9	CANNES	•	•	•	•							
10	ROUSSILLON	•	•	•	•			•				
11	VERDUN	•	•	•	•			•				
12	THE TOWER OF LONDON	•	•	•	•							
13	ANTWERP	•	•	•	•	•		•				
14	WESTMINSTER ABBEY	•	•	•	•	•						
15	THE SPANISH RIDING SCHOOL IN VIENNA	•	•	•	•	•						
16	FATIMA	•	•	•	•	•				•		
17	WINDSOR CASTLE	•	•	•	•	•					•	
18	THE OPAL COAST		•	•								
19	COTE D'AZUR	•	•	•	•	•						
20	AUSTRIA		•	•	•	•						
21	LOURDES	Currently being prepared										
22	BRUSSELS	•	•	•	•	•		•				
23	SCHÖNBRUNN PALACE	•	•	•	•	•		•				
24	ROUTE OF PORT WINE	•	•	•	•	•				•		
25	CYPRUS		•	•	•				•			
26	HOFBURG PALACE	•	•	•	•	•						
27	ALSACE	•	•	•	•	•		•				
28	RHODES		•	•	•							
29	BERLIN	Currently being prepared										
30	CORFU		•	•	•	•						
31	MALTA			•	•	•						
32	PERPIGNAN		•									
33	STRASBOURG	•	•	•	•	•						
34	MADEIRA	Currently being prepared										
35	CERDAGNE - CAPCIR		•				•					
36	CARCASSONE	Currently being prepared										
37	AVIGNON	Currently being prepared										

Collection ART IN SPAIN

		Spanish	French	English	German	Italian	Catalan	Dutch	Swedish	Portuguese	Japanese	Finnish
1	PALAU DE LA MUSICA CATALANA (Catalan Palace of Music)	Now being revised										
2	GAUDI	•	•	•	•	•					•	
3	PRADO MUSEUM I (Spanish Painting)	•	•	•	•	•					•	
4	PRADO MUSEUM II (Foreign Painting)	•	•	•	•	•						
5	MONASTERY OF GUADALUPE	•										
6	THE CASTLE OF XAVIER	•	•	•	•						•	
7	THE FINE ARTS MUSEUM OF SEVILLE	•	•	•	•	•						
8	SPANISH CASTLES	•	•	•	•							
9	THE CATHEDRALS OF SPAIN	•	•	•	•							
10	THE CATHEDRAL OF GERONA	•	•	•	•							
11	GRAN TEATRE DEL LICEU DE BARCELONA (The Great Opera House)	Now being revised										
12	THE ROMANESQUE STYLE IN CATALONIA	Currently being prepared										
13	LA RIOJA: ART TREASURES AND WINE-GROWING RESOURCES	•	•	•	•							
14	PICASSO	•	•	•	•	•					•	
15	REALES ALCAZARES (ROYAL PALACE OF SEVILLE)	•	•	•	•	•						
16	MADRID'S ROYAL PALACE	•	•	•	•	•						
17	ROYAL MONASTERY OF EL ESCORIAL	•	•	•	•	•						
18	THE WINES OF CATALONIA	•										
19	THE ALHAMBRA AND THE GENERALIFE	•	•	•	•	•						
20	GRANADA AND THE ALHAMBRA (ARAB AND MAURESQUE MONUMENTS OF CORDOVA, SEVILLE AND GRANADA)	•										
21	ROYAL ESTATE OF ARANJUEZ	•	•	•	•	•						
22	ROYAL ESTATE OF EL PARDO	•	•	•	•	•						
23	ROYAL HOUSES	•	•	•	•	•						
24	ROYAL PALACE OF SAN ILDEFONSO	•	•	•	•	•						
25	HOLY CROSS OF THE VALLE DE LOS CAIDOS	•	•	•	•	•						
26	OUR LADY OF THE PILLAR OF SARAGOSSA	•	•	•		•						

Collection ALL SPAIN

		Spanish	French	English	German	Italian	Catalan	Dutch	Swedish	Portuguese	Japanese	Finnish
1	ALL MADRID	•	•	•	•	•					•	
2	ALL BARCELONA	•	•	•	•	•	•					
3	ALL SEVILLE	•	•	•	•	•					•	
4	ALL MAJORCA	•	•	•	•	•						
5	ALL THE COSTA BRAVA	•	•	•	•	•						
6	ALL MALAGA and the Costa del Sol	•	•	•	•	•		•				
7	ALL THE CANARY ISLANDS, Gran Canaria, Lanzarote and Fuerteventura	•	•	•	•	•		•	•			
8	ALL CORDOBA	•	•	•	•	•					•	
9	ALL GRANADA	•	•	•	•	•		•			•	
10	ALL VALENCIA	•	•	•	•	•						
11	ALL TOLEDO	•	•	•	•	•					•	
12	ALL SANTIAGO	•	•	•	•	•						
13	ALL IBIZA and Formentera	•	•	•	•	•						
14	ALL CADIZ and the Costa de la Luz	•	•	•	•	•						
15	ALL MONTSERRAT	•	•	•	•	•	•					
16	ALL SANTANDER and Cantabria	•		•								
17	ALL THE CANARY ISLANDS II, Tenerife, La Palma, Gomera, Hierro	•	•	•	•	•		•	•			•
18	ALL ZAMORA	Currently being prepared										
19	ALL PALENCIA	Currently being prepared										
20	ALL BURGOS, Covarrubias and Santo Domingo de Silos	•	•	•	•	•						
21	ALL ALICANTE and the Costa Blanca	•	•	•	•	•		•				
22	ALL NAVARRA	•	•	•	•							
23	ALL LERIDA, Province and Pyrenees	•	•	•	•		•					
24	ALL SEGOVIA and Province	•	•	•	•	•						
25	ALL SARAGOSSA and Province	•	•	•	•	•						
26	ALL SALAMANCA and Province	•	•	•	•	•				•		
27	ALL AVILA and Province	•	•	•	•							
28	ALL MINORCA	•	•	•	•	•						
29	ALL SAN SEBASTIAN and Guipúzcoa	•										
30	ALL ASTURIAS	•		•								
31	ALL LA CORUNNA and the Rías Altas	•	•	•	•							
32	ALL TARRAGONA and Province	•	•	•	•	•						
33	ALL MURCIA and Province	•	•	•	•							
34	ALL VALLADOLID and Province	•	•	•	•							
35	ALL GIRONA and Province	•	•	•	•							
36	ALL HUESCA and Province	•	•									
37	ALL JAEN and Province	•	•	•	•							
38	ALL ALMERIA and Province	•	•	•	•							
39	ALL CASTELLON and the Costa del Azahar	Currently being prepared										
40	ALL CUENCA and Province	•	•	•	•							
41	ALL LEON and Province	•	•	•	•							
42	ALL PONTEVEDRA, VIGO and the Rías Bajas	•	•	•	•							
43	ALL RONDA	•	•	•	•	•						
44	ALL SORIA	•										
45	ALL HUELVA	Currently being prepared										
46	ALL EXTREMADURA	•										
47	ALL ANDALUSIA	•	•	•	•	•						
48	ALL GALICIA	Currently being prepared										
49	ALL CATALONIA	Currently being prepared										
50	ALL LA RIOJA	Currently being prepared										
51	ALL LUGO	Currently being prepared										
52	ALL MORELLA	•	•		•		•					

Collection ALL AMERICA

		Spanish	French	English	German	Italian	Catalan	Dutch	Swedish	Portuguese	Japanese	Finnish
1	PUERTO RICO	•		•								
2	SANTO DOMINGO	•		•								
3	QUEBEC		•	•								
4	COSTA RICA	•		•								

Collection ALL AFRICA

		Spanish	French	English	German	Italian	Catalan	Dutch	Swedish	Portuguese	Japanese	Finnish
1	MOROCCO	•	•	•	•	•						
2	THE SOUTH OF MOROCCO	•	•	•	•	•						
3	TUNISIA		•	•	•	•						

The printing of this book was completed in the workshops of FISA - Industrias Gráficas, Palaudarias, 26 - Barcelona (Spain)